I0142313

LITTLE VIANNE DISCOVERS CHRISTMAS

Written and illustrated by
Kerri Blache

Little Vianne Media
Mandeville, Louisiana

Published by Little Vianne Media
kerri@viannes.com
www.viannes.com

ISBN 979-8-9889658-0-0

Printed in the United States of America

Illustrations: Kerri Blache
Book design: Clarity Designworks

To my parents, Vianne and Lenny
with gratefulness.
And to my daughter, Chloë
who is even more beautiful than I could ever imagine.
And to my husband, Michael
who makes all my dreams come true.
With all my love!

FOREWORD

The butterfly is legend. These scaly-winged, day-flying insects have been idealized throughout the world's cultures and eras as the essence of beauty, the paragon of the natural world, and the "stuff of dreams." Endearing monikers include "Flying Jewels," "Dancing Flowers," and "Flowers of the Air." In addition, the butterfly is often considered the quintessential symbol and metaphor for transcendentalism, that is, a philosophy that embraces transformation, rebirth, renewal—put simply, change. Indeed, several Christian churches draft the butterfly image to represent the risen Christ on Easter Sunday. Finally, the butterfly image is commonly conscripted to be the logo for emotional support associations that champion life-changing experiences. All in all, much of the world's poetry, prose, art, music, and spiritual celebrations are all rife with the visage of the butterfly.

This iconic singularity derives from the butterfly's metamorphic life cycle: four distinct stages coded as egg, larva (caterpillar), pupa (chrysalis), and adult (butterfly). Each exclusive, each exceptional, and each appearing as if by magic.

With such a pedigree, it should come as no surprise that the butterfly has inspired humankind/s very psyche, aka "soul." And, it should come as no surprise, too, that Kerri Jones Blache selected the butterfly to represent **Little Vianne**, the protagonist in a new series of educational books for children. The nexus between an innocent, curious child and a rare, beautiful butterfly is perfect for discovery, and for the retelling of iconic Jesusonian tales laced with humankind's spiritual passion for tea. And readers, regardless of age, are granted a glimpse of their personal, final metamorphosis into eternal bliss.

Gary Noel Ross, Ph.D.
Butterfly Scientist
June 2023

Gary Noel Ross, Ph.D. is a retired Professor of Biological Sciences, Southern University. He has spent his life researching not only the scientific aspect of butterflies, but how butterflies and diverse human cultures interact on a mythological and spiritual basis .Dr. Ross makes Baton Rouge his home base. There, he maintains a large butterfly garden to educate himself as well as his neighbors and visitors.

Hello My Dear Friend,

My name is Little Vianne, and I am no ordinary butterfly! My wings sparkle in the sunlight. I love to fly high and far, watching the wonders of our world. I see things others might miss—like secrets hidden in flowers, rivers that sing, and stories of long ago.

In this book, I want to share one of my favorite discoveries: The First Christmas! It was a charming home, special love, and the miracle of birth like all tiny babies!

I was there to see it with my friend Lovin' Lenny—he's a mighty firefly. We fluttered and flew around mountains and trees. Now, I'm excited to tell you everything we learned!

As you turn the pages, imagine us flying beside you (like unseen angels) showing you the way. Please join us in this adventure of discovery. Remember—wherever you go, you can always find God's love shining, just like the glisten on my wings and the glow of Lenny's tail!

With love and fluttery hugs,
Little Vianne

Little Vianne is a rare and beautiful butterfly. She always is and always shall be. She has long eyelashes and her color is petal pink with glimmery gold spots—called eyespots (to ward off predators).

Little Vianne never had any problem with predators. She prayed often for protection for her friends, family and herself.

Before each journey, I pause to pray,
"God, please guide me along the way"

Little Vianne likes tea and tea parties. Vianne's best friend is Lenny; a friendly and mighty firefly nicknamed *Lovin' Lenny*.

We sip our tea, then off we go,
To places from long, long ago.

Little Vianne is a curious butterfly. She loves to flit about the gardens in lovely Nazareth while observing all the interesting happenings. She loved Mary—ever since Mary was a little girl. Mary was smart, did well with her studies and was a good planner. Little Vianne liked to sit quietly and read.

One day, while sipping tea, Little Vianne saw it happen—Joseph and Mary met! She did not know it was special then but does now. Mary's father had Joseph work to build an addition to their house. He was a skilled carpenter and a real thinker. It was during a noontime meal that Mary brought Joseph a cup of water and their eyes met.

Little Vianne, being an observant butterfly for a long time, knew **that was the look of love. Real love, kind love, lasting love—God's love.**

In the springtime, Joseph and Mary were married, in a Jewish custom, at Mary's home in Nazareth.

This marriage concluded a normal courtship of almost two years' duration, when Joseph was twenty-one years old. Little Vianne helped Mary pick the prettiest and most fragrant flowers for her bridal head wreath and wore one too!

They moved into their new home in Nazareth, which was built by Joseph and two of his brothers. The house was located near the foot of the nearby elevated land, which so charmingly overlooked the surrounding countryside. Little Vianne loved taking care of the flowers and watching them bloom with Mary.

One evening about sundown, before Joseph had returned home, Gabriel appeared to Mary by the side of a low stone table, and it took a few moments for Mary to understand and see clearly. Little Vianne noticed a glow coming from the cottage and flew to the window with haste.

Little Vianne heard it all! She told Lenny that the angel said:

I come at the bidding of one who is my Master and whom you shall love and nurture. To you, Mary, I bring glad tidings when I announce that the baby within you is blessed by heaven, and that in due time you will become the mother of a son; you shall call him Jesus.

Mary thought about the angel's visit for many weeks until she knew she was with child and then she told Joseph about the unusual visit and mighty words. Little Vianne was so happy to hear Joseph and Mary talk about this serious matter. There was concern but love in their voices.

When Joseph heard all about this, he could not sleep for many nights. At first, Joseph had doubts about the angel Gabriel's visit. Then when he felt that Mary had really heard the voice and saw an angel, after several weeks of thought, both he and Mary reached the conclusion that they had been chosen to become the parents of the Messiah.

Joseph had a very impressive dream. In this dream, the angel appeared to him too and said many things including: *"Joseph, I am directed to instruct you concerning the son whom Mary shall bear, and who shall become a great light in the world."* After this experience, Joseph believed Mary's story of Gabriel's visit.

Around this time, Caesar Augustus said everyone should enroll in a census.

It was not necessary that Mary should go to Bethlehem for enrollment—Joseph could register for his family—but Mary, being an adventurous and aggressive person, insisted on going too. She feared being left alone lest the child be born while Joseph was away. Little Vianne could not wait to take a trip and was packed and ready before Mary!

The next morning, Joseph and Mary cheerfully departed from Nazareth at the break of day. Little Vianne finished her prayers, told Lenny goodbye and was ready to go by dawn.

Joseph and Mary were poor, and since they had only one donkey, Mary, being large with child, rode on the animal while Joseph walked, leading the beast. They left from their humble home early, on their journey to Bethlehem.

Their first day of travel carried them around the foothills of Mount Gilboa, where they camped for the night by the river Jordan and talked about what sort of a son would be born to them. Little Vianne was so tired; she fell asleep immediately in her comfy leaf tent even with the shooting stars above!

Bright and early in the morning, Joseph and Mary were again on their way to Bethlehem. They had their noontide meal at the foot of Mount Sartaba, overlooking the Jordan valley, and journeyed on, making Jericho for the night, where they stopped at an inn on the highway in the outskirts of the city.

Donkeys
in
Back

Little Vianne loved chatting with a warm and welcoming new friend. Following the evening meal and after much discussion concerning world events, the Nazareth travelers retired for the night's rest.

Early in the morning they resumed their journey, reaching Jerusalem before noon, visiting the temple, and going on to their destination. Little Vianne was mesmerized by the colorful stained glass window and did not want to leave!

Arriving at Bethlehem in midafternoon, the inn was overcrowded, and every room in Bethlehem was filled to overflowing. At the courtyard of the inn, Joseph was told that the caravan stables, hewn out of the side of the rock and situated just below the inn, had been cleared of animals and cleaned up for lodgers.

Leaving the donkey in the courtyard, Joseph and Mary descended the stone steps. They counted themselves fortunate to have such comfortable quarters. Little Vianne felt so happy to see that Lenny was already there!

Joseph had thought to go out at once and enroll in the census, but Mary was weary and asked him to remain by her side, which he did. Little Vianne and friends said their prayers for Mary and baby then fell fast asleep.

With the help of kind women fellow travelers, Mary was delivered of a male child. Jesus of Nazareth was born into the world, was wrapped in the clothes that Mary thought to bring along and laid in a nearby manger. Lenny and Little Vianne were awe-struck. They had never seen such a tiny newborn baby before.

In just the same manner as all babies before that day and since have come into the world, the promised child was born; and named Jesus.

Baby
Jesus
is
beautiful

At the birth of Jesus, all the angels sang anthems of glory over the Bethlehem manger, but these songs were not heard by human ears.

The First Christmas was born!

Weeks later, priests from Ur came to visit to honor and celebrate the blessed and momentous event of the universe.

Little Vianne wishes all a
"Merry Christmas!"

Glossary

Anthem – a rousing or uplifting song identified with a particular cause.

Bidding – the ordering or requesting of someone to do something.

Caravan stables – a place where animals and equipment are stored for traveling by camels or donkeys, historically pack animals.

Census – an official count or survey of a population, typically recording various details of individuals.

Courtship – a period during which a couple develop a romantic relationship, especially with a view to marriage.

Descended – to be on a slope or incline and extend downward.

Destination – the place to which someone or something is going or being sent.

Enroll – officially register.

Eyespot – a rounded eye-like marking on an animal, especially on the wing of a butterfly or moth.

Glad tidings – good news.

Hewn – chopped or cut.

Journey – an act of traveling from one place to another.

Lodgers – a person who occupies a rented room.

Manger – a long open box or trough for horses or cattle to eat from.

Messiah – the promised deliverer of the Jewish nation prophesied in the Hebrew Bible. The Hebrew Bible is a collection of writings that was first compiled and preserved as the sacred books of the Jewish people.

Momentous – of great importance or significance, especially in its bearing on the future.

Nurture – care for and encourage the growth or development of.

Observant – quick to notice things.

Personified – made to seem like a real person. Little Vianne and Lovin' Lenny are make believe.

Predator – an animal that naturally preys on others.

Skilled – having or showing the knowledge, ability or training to perform a certain activity or task well.

About the Author

Kerri Jones Blache is a development professional with New Orleans PBS affiliate station, WYES-TV/PBS for thirty years. She also owned and operated an international teahouse for 13 years and still has Vianne's Teas online, where "Little Vianne's Tea" can be found—www.viannes.com.

Kerri lives in a charming and historic lakeside town just north of New Orleans with her family where she enjoys reading, writing and tea—almost daily!

With a sip of tea and a prayer to start,
Little Vianne and Lovin' Lenny light the heart.
Come discover God's wonders with me—
In the Spirituali-TEA Discovery Series!

Help Little Vianne and Lovin' Lenny choose teacups
from around the world!